Ahmed Nasr Morsy

One Hundred Philo-Poems
At the age of Twenty-six

Edited
By
Harte Weiner, PHD

One Hundred Philo-Poems
At The age of Twenty Six

One Hundred Philo-Poems At The age of Twenty Six

Ahmed N. Morsy

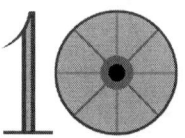

Morsy's Vision of Hope Books

New York

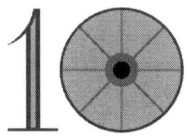

Morsy's Vision of Hope Books

New York

Published in the United States

By Morsy's Vision of Hope Books

553 w 144th st, apt 12 New York, New York 10031, USA

www.Ahmedmorsy.com

(917) 994 0083

(347) 805 5258

Cover Design by Ahmed N. Morsy and Santiago Peralta

Copyright© Ahmed Morsy 2012

All rights reserved. No part of this publication may be reproduced or utilized in any form or by any mechanical, electronic, or other means, without prior permission in writing from the publisher.

Printed in New York

ISBN:9781480166219

Acknowledgements

I want to give the biggest thanks to God for being my protector and guide on my journey on planet earth. I want to thank my wife for making me a father, a better man, supporting me, and sharing wonderful moments together through all negativity. I want to thank all the educators and mentors I had in Evander Childs High School in the north Bronx, Eugenio María de Hostos community college in the South Bronx, and at John Jay College of criminal justice in the heart of New York City. Especial gratitude goes to my favorite professor Dr. Hernando Estévez, a philopher at John Jay College of criminal justice who positively influenced my life as a student, father, husband, and as a human being. I also want to thank Dr. Harte Weiner for being the editor of my book and for her advice on how to improve as a young writer. I want to thank all the athletes that I trained, played with in high school, college, the streets of Honduras, and the United States. I am very thankful to Santiago Peralta an alumni, Eugenio María de Hostos community college, who transferred my art to digital format. Lastly I want to thank Maya, Jillian, my family, staff and residents at North Bronx group home for contributing to the person I am today.

Dedicated to:

The oppressed and less fortuned around the universe.

Contents

Philo-poetry 1

Summary of my Biography 3

My Children 9

Mother 10

Father 11

Glory in your Adversity 12

Authenticity 13

Adversity over Fortune 14

For Love 15

Victim of Circumstances 16

Evil 17

Abstraction 18

Mental State 19

Because of Necessity Harm 20

Bad Environment 21

Sun 22

Fight of Thoughts 23

Laughter   24

Reality of Tears   25

Harmony   26

Indifference   27

The massage   28

Communication   29

Brain   30

To Share   31

Always Positive   32

To Control the Tongue   33

Enthusiasm   34

You Are   35

Always in Company   36

Salvation in Art   37

Conscious   38

You and Your Truth   39

Aesthetic   40

Optimism with Pain   41

Nature   42

New Lights   43

Acts   44

Depression   45

Something to Live   46

Justice   47

Song of fútbal   48

Education   50

Perseverance   51

Detail   52

Miss   53

To Comprehend Humanity   54

The Creator   55

Pupils   56

Sleep   57

Risk   58

Intellect between the Ignorant   59

Orders   60

Pleasures   61

Competitions   62

Envy   63

Advice   64

Compassion   65

Equality   66

Expected meeting   67

Extremism   68

Explanations   69

Atheist believer   70

Much   71

Cruel Universe   72

The Law   73

Suffering   74

Women   75

Go to Sleep My Children   76

Patience is Medicine   77

Magic   78

Supreme Voice   79

Divine Vision   80

Reality   81

Time to Act   82

Hope   83

Disaster   84

Humble Confidence   85

Allergic to Problems   86

Everything is a Blessing   87

Thankful   88

Something Historical   89

Before is too Late   90

Clear or Not   91

Confusion   92

Free Will   93

Honesty   94

I believe in your Heart   95

In Lows with Us   96

Moment of Love   97

Observe my Truth   98

Special Day   99

Step of Righteous Faith   100

The Childhood   101

The Negotiator   102

The Rich Poverty   103

To have Power   104

Trap in Love   105

Without Understanding   106

You gave me Strengths   107

Silence   108

Philo-Poetry - Analysis, wisdom, and life experiences that develop internal feelings with the purpose of helping humanity and all its surroundings.

Summary of my Biography

I was born in Brascia, Italy, on August 30, 1985. My Birth name is Ahmed Nasr Ahmed Aly Morsy. My father was born in Egypt and my mother in Honduras. They fell in love and married in Italy. My father name is Nasr Ahmed Aly Morsy, and my mother's name is María Antonia Martinez Erazo. My father's first language is Arabic and my mother's Spanish, they communicated in Italian. When I was one year old my parents took me to Alexandria, Egypt where my father and his family are from; when I was two years old and for reasons unknown, though, my mother took me out of Egypt and brought me to Honduras without my father. The reason and facts for this is a mystery to me—over the phone and in writing, my mother has told that she will explain one day; but only in person. When I was four years old my mother immigrated to the United States.

From the age of four to thirteen, I was raised by my hard working grandmother, Raquel María Erazo who raised nine children and over 20 grandchildren. Even though Honduras is one of the poorest and most corrupt nations in the world, my childhood in Honduras was full of joy. I played soccer and other sports most of the day, swam at the beach, and I sold lottery to help my grandmother financially—helping her made me feel really good. Everybody in Honduras wants to come to the United States for many positive factors; back home we hear of the affluence and opportunities of the United States. While I described my childhood as idyllic in Honduras, around me I saw violence, crimes and drugs. I credit my grandmother for being very strict and hard on me and my other cousins when we stole as kids, and for instilling in us that we should respect our elders.

When I immigrated to the United States my brain was not fully developed. I did not understand that I was breaking the law and that the future consequences would be full of adversity, inequality, and suffering--just to preserve my life. I confess that it has been a struggle to stay righteous and lawful, while being undocumented. The reality is that in order to survive, and avoid personal exploitation; you might have to break the law. Although you wish to stay within the law, you do not want to become a victim. I did fear becoming useless and incompetent in a great nation. Before I left Honduras, and was living my grandmother, aunts and cousins, I viewed the road to American as the escape from violence, and from poverty, as the opportunity for a better future.

On September 15th 1998, Honduran Independence day, I told my grandmother that I was heading to the United States, and on the 16th of the same month the journey started .It was right before hurricane Mitch, one of the worst in the history of Central America and Honduras. Crossing the brave river that divides Texas and Mexico took me a month. This Journey is in me for the rest of my life. The trip consisted of walking for hours in cold and burning conditions, longs hours in back of a truck with little comfort;, dangerous speed boats, thirst, hunger and plenty of dirty water to drink and for showering. We had to sleep in mountains, sand and grass for different nights, and many of us were bitten by different animals, especially mosquitoes, and scorpions. I was part of a group of roughly 60, made up of children, adolescents and adults, and we were guided my smugglers who I believe meant no harm. We crossed tree borders--the one between Guatemala and Honduras, Guatemala and Mexico, and Mexico and U.S. This is one of the reasons they called Hondurans ' "three times illegal."

I landed in Manhattan New York on a cold October night of 1998. I was in shock by the sides of the building, the lights and the people. I found New York City alluring; and, while my uncle and cousins were in the way to pick me up, I got lost in the madness of the city. It hit me fast. I was so innocent that I appreciated the details of the city that today I take for granted, though I shouldn't.

Once picked up, I was left to Brooklyn to live with my aunt and cousins. I lived with my aunt Silvia and some of my cousins ages 13 to 15. In early 2001, I was placed in foster care or a group Home called "North Bronx," where I resided with 11 other adolescents and young adults who been abuse or neglected. I was place there by the family court of New York. I was under Salvation Army who was under the Administration for Children's Services (ACS). The reason for this was design by me for my wellbeing. I was admitted in a group home under the name of Anthony Estevez—which I called my artistic name, since it is not my birth name. I thought my name was irrelevant at that moment because I had no documents, and no ways of getting anything, such as my birth certificate. The group home had structure but it was not designed for undocumented people like me. The purpose of the program was to help adolescents prepare for adulthood and to get independent in the near future. We were allowed to stay until the age of 21. Part of the structure was for us to work and save money to be prepared for the real world. Another goal was to provide housing, section 8, public assistance, and financial aid to go to college. I could not work or qualify for any of these programs, however, because of my immigration status; so I decided to scalp tickets to safe money so I can become independent, attend college and pursue a Liberal Arts education.

Scalping tickets is a violation, not a crime. Still, between the ages of 17 and 25 I got over 100 arrests. These arrests caused me a lot of suffering and also the surprising chance to adjust my immigration status. I was doing it for necessity; but, the immigration attorney who was provided to me advised me not to apply for a Juvenile visa (SIJ) because my arrests. Although I got arrested all these times, I managed to get an associate's degree in Liberal Arts (AA) from Eugenio María de Hostos, and to continue at John Jay College of Criminal Justice, where I am pursuing a bachelors (BA) in Philosophy with a minor in Art. Mrs. Best was (and hope still is) an elderly old lady, then 82 years old, who allowed me to clean and take care of her garden and helped me while I was in foster care, especially with words of wisdom. Her favorite's words to me were "You are going to be a big shot; I need your autograph so I can say I knew you." I had a great relationship with her and when I aged out of the group home, she and her brother rented me the second floor of her home across the street from the group home.

On a May evening, and while coming from scalping my tickets, I saw the most beautiful women in the world, Christie Aracelis Rosario. I remember that date as if it were today. God gave me the right words to approach her. She was well spoken, and had a beautiful smile. Alicia Keys came up in the conversation and we exchange numbers. We spoke over the phone, we dated and to me, she was sent from heaven. Since the first time I saw her, she filled my heart with a beautiful sensation; I never called it *love* because I did not know what love was. Now I can acknowledge that I loved her since that first date, on the 4 train. By August 27th of the same year I was getting marry to the most beautiful women in the world, my first girlfriend my first and only authentic love.

Reviewing the past, we both did everything fast and irresponsibly, not considering the effect that our actions were going to cost ourselves and others. My wife wants to make her parents proud of her, and I hope they see how hard she is trying to make up for her mistakes. I firmly believe that our intentions were good and that we did not meant to hurt anyone. Our actions caused ourselves a lot of harm also. On July 23rd 2009 our first daughter Aracelis María Aly Morsy was born, and on August 9th 2010 Emmanuel Nasr Aly Morsy was born. I am attached to my wife since the first day I met her I love her, and I love my children since they were in her wound. While we faced all types of adversities, my wife Christie is my hope, Aracelis my faith, and Emmanuel my strength. Christie came into my life and game me hope, Aracelis was planned because of our faith that God would provide for us, and Emmanuel is my first son and sign of strength we have. Our relationship had a lot of up and downs over the years and we hurt each other. I acknowledge my mistakes and I agree with her that I have to get my act together, be a good influence for my children and, that I should provide for them. My love for her is authentic, and I forgive her, I believe in her, I respect her, I appreciate her, and her work, in the house, school, and her future job. I am optimistic that she will one day appreciate my effort to become her perfect man.

I am writing a book whose purpose is rooted in helping humanity and all its surroundings: I feel good that my words from within can help others. For me it is also a creative way to legally perform my human right of preserving my life without breaking the law. While my purpose is to help others, the book also helps me. This book positions me to resolve my immigration status, get a career and offer society and my love ones a better human being.

I pray to God that he turns our weaknesses, adversity, pain-- our loneliness, hunger, thirst, depression and injustices--into our strength. I also hope that with this book I can help others overcome some adversities caused by this unjust universe. I am undocumented,

I lived in foster care, I experienced prison, lived in a shelter and I even placed myself in a comprehensive psychiatric emergency program when I was exhausted by the pains of life. With the help of God, I am turning all my adversities, pains and weaknesses into my strength to fulfill the purpose I have and I believe we all have.

We will never lose hope, Ahmed N.Morsy

1-My children

Cute at birth

More precious each day

It inspires me

The blessing of your existence

You are the fruit of the love I have

For the same person

You also love

Never forget

The reality of being able to obtain

Whatever you proposed

Patient is a virtue

Perseverance is another

You will be influence

By your generic attributes

Normally your environments

Education is a shield

Powerful

Against

The malice

Shine between the good

2- Mother

Creation

In which we owed eternal love

Internal and external love

Minimum

The most sweet and lovely beautiful words

Of the universal dictionaries

From kids to adults

We have to show them gratitude

They have to count on us

For everything that have

A positive impact

In the complete picture

That reflects both

Including others

Female is to us

What we are to God

God

Thank you for her

Mother (María)

Thank you for everything

3-Father

Father like my father

Men like my father

Do I think like my father?

Do I love like my father?

I experienced, I am experiencing, and will I experience the same as my father?

I will always remember my father

I want to honor you father

Thank you father

4- Glory in your adversity

The more adversities you overcame

More value you have in society

Value of experiences not superiority

If the measurements are just

Your sufferings, struggles, accomplishments, and sacrifices

Are deserving of merit and recognition

From the best supreme judges universally

The question is not, how far you got?

The question is, how you were able to get to where you got?

Taking in consideration

Your supports and life tools

Five miles running by feet

Are more valuable than twenty by car

Towards the good

 Pure principle

Of a good heart

5- Authenticity

To be authentic or real with actions

Is almost impossible

For necessities, designs, and life structures

With our minds, and feelings

We can always be authentic

By being honest

With ourselves

6- Adversity over fortune

Because our adversities we are humble

For your fortunes you are lordly

We flew low with our own wings

You flew very high

With inherited or borrowed wings

Everything is mathematics

7- For love

Sacrifice everything

Except your believe in God

If you do not believe in him

Observe nature or the perfect circle of you pupils

For real love

Your life you will give

In body, soul, and spirit

Love

I love you

Honestly

8- **Victim of circumstances**

We born in conditions

To fail

Our environments are negatives

We accomplished to escape and succeed

Now we are confronting

The injustices of the universe

This realism cause us suffering

Which will be recompensed

By God

9- Evil

It's cruel existence is real

Actions in its name

Results in suffering and severe consequences

We have to get isolated from perversities

10- Abstraction

Pure imagination

Which can convert the unjust universe

In a place

Perfectly just

With lines, colors, shapes or any medium

You decide to use

It has the power to give you the happiness

That you will never find in realism

11- Mental state

Fundamentally important

To determine you stability

Mentally, physically, *sexually*, financially, and educative

Develop a technique

To maintain control

Of your mental state

12-Because of necessity harm

Necessity cause, caused, and will cause harm

For its own nature of necessity

Is unjust to measure any wrong doing

Without measuring the requirement

13 -Bad environment

It puts your present and future in danger

Be strong against its negative influence

Do not allow it to transform you

In someone of malice

Is a fight with the genetics

The good will triumph

14 -Sun

You come out, in, and shine

Never discriminate

Under you

Things of every type of dimensions walked, walk, and will walk

You have good judgment

In your eyes

We all are

Equal

15- Fight of thoughts

So many at once

Is a fight to give one a priority

What I should or I should not think

This one is good and the other is bad

One makes us feel sad and the other happy

You focus in one, but is the wrong one

You realize that is the wrong one

The fight continues

16 –Laughter

It has secrets

Of harmony, happiness, and peace

With humor is exploited

It shares pleasures

Do not abandon us

We want to express all

Our laughter

17-Reality of tears

The truth of the real present

That what you love the most

Does not love you anymore and even

You are something abominable for its humanity

Now It gets you mentally sick

It harms you physically

You ask God

For it not to eat from the resentments

It blames you for the errors and failures of both

Ignores your devotion

To fight for the authentic love

In reality you have for him/her

This causes your heart

To ache in an inexplicable way with words

If this is your truth

Tears will come out of your eyes

In the same form

That you come out your house

18-Harmony

Sister of peace

To live with you

Is a healthy pleasure

We crave you with open arms

When you are absent

The agony is present

You are welcome

All the time

19-Indifference

Every creation is unique

The indifferent interpretations

Are done

Impossible to ignore

Let's tolerate and accept

Our points of view

Is fundamentally

To coexist

In harmony

20-The message

Is communication in a notice

Announced in a message

Not always will be by the best role models

To analyze it well is the purpose

If someone malicious tells you

Say no to malice

Listen to the message

Judge it and be thankful for what was learned

21-Communication

Essential in the world of peace

Is a guarantee ticket

To the paradise of the harmony of home

There exist the responsibility of varies parts

One fails

The team failed

22- Brain

Ball with treasures inside

Inimitable creation

Exceptionally distinct

It accomplishes things every day more surprising

Root

Of the creativity

23-To share

To give of your misery

Is something immense

To have in affluence

But share it with no one

Is to have little

To want to give in shortage

Is more than give it all

24- Always positive

In agony, happiness, prison or freedom

Let's focus on optimism

Of all the acts

It died

It hurt us

Think that it left to a better universe

Convert its absence and our pains

In strengths

We lost the prices

But we won

Because we gave

Our best

25-To control the tongue

Once we tame the little pink ant

We have self-power

It has destructive potential

Without control of it

The tragedy is

A matter of time

26- Enthusiasm

Dazzle a mix

Of motivation and inspiration

In present and future actions

Honest attitude

Optimistic smile

Time well spent

Acts remembered

Activities realized

Correctly

27-You are

My most nutritious diet

The pupils of my eyes

The tongue of my mouth

The flowers of my spring

My authentic love

Which suffers because of the reality

Of moments of separation

You the spirit of my soul

The mind and heart of my body

The purpose of these words

Are to be the oxygen in your blood

For when you run you do not get fatigue

Take my bread, chicken and pizza

Seven times

Than paint me red

I will say

You are

My Best, like A and E

28-Always in company

Is with you always

Your loneliness is as abstract as is real

The presence will not be touch, visible, feel, or enjoy

Understand that we are all

Eternally accompanied

By God

29-Salvation in art

To paint, sing, write, read, dance, or play

Can be activities of emotional expressions

Which we use in good or difficult times

It causes a harmonic therapy

To preserve art is a universal responsibility

Your art or whatever we consider art

Can save our lives,

And much more

30-conscious

Present remorse

In some more than others

We can lie to our selves

But not to her

We have to be at peace with our thoughts

If not

The suffering is constant and internal

31-You and your truth

Only God can know you like your self

Nobody else has that power

Be honest with yourself

Without being prideful or sensitive

With the conclusions

That others determine towards, who you are?

Many will commit errors

Because your appearances and actions

God and you know the truth

Celebrate that detail

32 -Aesthetic

We are unique

We interpret and feel differently

Our treasures

Is your garbage, and vice versa

Our perception has the right

To originality

We must respect the conclusions of others

Based on aesthetic

33-Optimism with pain

Sign of strengths

Examination passed with honors

The redemption was possible

With the help of the creator and creation

We got the blessing

Of maintaining optimistic with pain

Now

Let's humbly be positive

Towards everything our ways

34- Nature

Naturally pure form

Example of a creator or supreme architect

With powers not reachable by men or women

Beautiful originality and admirable

Details perfected

We have to be careful with her

It is a tool

Neutral

35-New light

In times of a lot darkness

Permanent light will come

To remind us

That God loves us

Let's tuck in that love

And allow it

To perform good

To us and others

36-Acts

Impacts they had, have, and will have

For some good and others bad

The attitude towards you

Will be the effects

Of our cause

37-Depression

Crucial sinking

With despair

It provides metal and physical pain

It has potential of a tragedy

Optimistic hope and faith

Is fundamental

We will diminish it

Little by little

God will assist us

38-Something to live

Our reasons to not wanting to live

Have to be our strengths

To live with purposes

We have to convert

Our adversities, pains, failures, and sickening feelings

In our most powerful

Attributes and resources

39-Justice

Plenty of different notions

About what is in reality

Let's question the acts

For its existence universally

We most declares its absence

Acting authentically

Base in our original philosophy

On, what is justice?

For us

We are unique

We think and interpret different

For me

Justice is

The guarantee of equality in every circumstance measure equally

Mathematically

40-Song of fútbal

Let's forget war

Let's forget religion

Let's forget nations

Let's forget history today, and let's play fútbal

Let's play fútbal

Let's play fútbal

Let's play fútbal

Let's play fútbal

Optimistic game

Intellectual game

Brotherly game

Strategic game

Passionate game

Just game

Humane game

Is the game of life

Let's play fútbal

Let's play fútbal

Let's play fútbal

Let's play fútbal

Is ear of the deaf

Word of the dumb

Eyes of the blind

Water for the thirsty

Food for the hungry

Is pure humanity

Is the game of life

Let's play fútbal

Let's play fútbal

Let's play fútbal

Let's play fútbal

41 -Education

Dedication fundamental

With promises of development

Magically incredible

It shares keys

To the human triumph

It provides wisdom, humbleness, and universal understanding

Of humanity and its surroundings

We must educate ourselves

The most we can

42 -Perseverance

We failed, we failed, and we failed

Now we have to maintain firmly endeavor

With consistent tenacity

To our purpose

When obstacles are present

Your motivation can not be absent

Failed exams

Eventually will be passing

The door to our destiny

Continue to knock it

43-Detail

Thingy little thing

Minimum observation

Immensely appreciated

With perfect vision

Hands moving and feet walking

Form of chew and sleep

Value

Absolutely thankful

In everything

In our focus

44-Miss

It put us

In a depressive state

It rob us the happiness and energy

Loneliness harass us

Our thirst is as constant as the change of time

The days are too long or too short

We do not find satisfaction with anything

Our present is affected

By the past

That promised a future

Far instead of near

45-To comprehend humanity

It's a fantasy to give general answers

About all type of people

Some give it all and some take it all

Our purposes have different intentions

The more we study life

The more we understand it

The more we understand humanity

We will conclude in a mixed reality

Some want to perform well

And others have pride in doing evil

Some seek materialism

Others search

Love and peace

46 - The creator

Is called

"The architect of the universe"

By great thinkers and scholars of life

Is the most just judge towards what can be

He is with all of us

We must not let him go

In happiness or sorrow

Abundance or shortage

Unconditional loyalty

Is our minimum act

Of gratitude

47- Pupils

Honest impression

A lot of times wrongly interpret

Clue to comprehend

The intentions

Of others

48- Sleep

To do it without obstacles is peace

Preoccupation is its enemy

Harmony and fatigue its ally

We have to think little or nothing

Tomorrow is another day

Now

We owe the responsibility

To rest

To our home

The body

49-Risk

Act of faith

Hope and necessity

For inexplicable emptiness

Its result

Is an optimistic anxiety

Our reason is our purpose

Is time to resolve

It's a duty

To died or overcome

God

Guide us

50- Intellect between the ignorant

There exist all types of intellects and ignorance

The responsibility of the intellect

Is to help the ignorant

By sharing, influencing and living

With the ignorance of any type or dimension

The educated purpose

Is to convert in a reality

A more productive help for the universal society

The intellect is the humbleness that is missing from the pride fullness of ignorance

51-Oders

Leaders had to support them

Soldiers are loyal to them

Employers demand them

Our authenticity suffers

Because our conditions and necessity

Let's not be rebels or sensitive

We must prepare and obtain resources

For our Purpose

52-Pleasures

To see the sun come out and go in

To listen to the sea waves

To walk or run behind a ball

To coexist with our love ones

To study life and accept its unjust reality

To have compassion for others

To visualize our correct vision of hope

Imagining that is not only a dream

To be at peace with our conscience

Finally

To convert in one

With the person we love

53- Competition

The best is

When the competition

Is our selves

Looking for new results

Is the thirst to our potential

It is related with envy

For the nature to want to occupy

A Place already another's

Conflict with each other

In competition

We must think we are the best

With our heart, mind, physical, soul, and spirit

Let's defeat

Our own competition

54-Envy

To course

The ones that have

Whatever we want

Is deserving of a big punishment

If God orders it

We must learn from them

Let's applaud them and respect them

They are in that position

Because a family foundation, merit or plenty

Of self-sacrifice

55- Advice

From who or where it comes (from)

It has great value

Some more than others for its contents

The worse tips can be clues

To your destination

Let's take advantage of them

Keeping in mind

How propaganda

Works

56-Compassion

To feel the pains and penalties of others

Is a war against the suffering

Which is constant in the reality of the earth

Let's not jeer of the sadness, sorrow or bitterness

Of others

We must be part of them

57- Equality

Procreated equally

Now we must be measure in circumstances and situation identically

Different wisdom and attributes

To balance the human talents

Notions of superiority

Are truthful ignorance

Without pureness in the heart, brain, and feelings

Equality is a magical fruit

Of good Judgment

58- Expected meeting

When God wants

It will come

It will be a night

With full moon and countable of stars

The separated will unite like a magnet

We will naturally be together

The sun will give a beautiful welcome

To a sweet morning

Hoping

For the perfect afternoon

To walk

Around beauty

59-Extremism

To never be one is the purpose

We have to accept our differences with others

Let's not grasp in our points of view

Without considering the ones of others

If we decide to become one

What type is fundament (ally)

We must grow as humans

By living in harmony

Of heart

60- Explanations

To give them is respect

We cannot see them as excuses all the time

They are examples of the importance of the matter

It is transparent

To accept fault

To be thankful for them

Is Mature

61-Atheist believer

They declare verbally

They doubt in God

But their actions

Worship him

A lot of us manifest our belief in Him

It is clear that our conducts

Express the opposite

There are atheist believers

In God

For reasons

Of actions and pure

Intentions

62- Much

We lost the limits

We forgot the measurements

The judgments escaped

Now we face the consequences

Less in our case

Could have been

Perfect

63- Cruel universe

For its nature, environment, and generics

Will hit us strongly

Our physical, mind, soul, and spirit

Let's devote our energies

To help our conditions and the ones of others

We have to stay authentic towards the good

Pure principle

Of a good heart

64-The Law

What is the purpose of the law?

This question has to be the core of the discussion of every law

By nature

Our interpretations will be different

Once we agree with the purpose

We can Apply it more effective and justly

65-Suffering

Happiness despises you

Your rebellion is constant in humanity

You result because compassion

You adore tears

It is a war

Physically, and mentally

In the reality of life

You win

But in the abstraction

We defeated you

66-Women

Strong by nature

Some bad like taxis

When the weather is bad it's hard to find one

Let show them acts of love

Like listening and beautiful forms to treat them

We should never separate them from their love ones

We have to find a sweet one with a lot of love to give

With tremendous family value

The one that will want to marry

67-Go to sleep my children

Go to sleep my children

Go to sleep with God

Papi and mami Loves you

Loves you a lot

Princes and prince of our empire

Most valuable treasures

Light of our eyes

Love of our loves

68- Patience is medicine

Everything that we want now

To have in the moment is impossible

Do we torture ourselves or we get calm and wait

It requires experience and wisdom

It evolves human development

69- Magic

Is an artistic science

Hidden in invisibly transparent secrets

Is energy abstractly real

Mathematical results

With fruit of hope

For all

70- Supreme Voice

It guides us in a special form

Our conduct is natural

The tiredness is ignore

We drink patience and perseverance

We eat hope and faith

Its existence

Is a truth

71- Divine vision

Clearly invisible

A just mission

Project perfected

Secret geometry

Code of the peace

72- Reality

Truth of

Hard acceptance

But it's a necessity

Ignorance is not an excuse

Once we get educated we've succeeded

In our failed reality

Our reality is sophisticated

With optimism and sacrifice

Our reality has potential

To accomplish

Our purposes

73- Time to act

Present is the moment

Our patience was very long

We have to demonstrate our preparation

Let's control our nerves and fears

God is with us

We most focus in our purpose

The result will be compensated

By God

74-Hope

Is the spark

To a purpose connected with destiny

Brain of the universal faith

Blind goodness

Intimate feelings

Highly expressed

From within

75- Disaster

Why?

We do not have ask

We have to act

With help in our reach

The physical harm

Blood in abundance

Hearts stopped

Souls flying

We have to be part of the pains

Without any discrimination

In minimum detail

In dark acts

We most bring light

To others and then us

76-Humble confidence

We know ourselves

In us we believe

Nerves and fears we faced

Critics we ignored

But learned from them

Our minds are stable

Our conscious at peace

If we put our head down is humbleness

Not insecurity

77- Allergic to problems

Don't look or desire problems

Let's avoid dilemmas

We have to face and solve our problems

Talking is a good technique

When they are present

We have to live them as fast as we can

Our gratitude

For not having problems

78- Everything is a blessing

The worse that happened to us

Contributed

To our human growth

We born with blessings

Our surrounding are a blessing

Let's open our eyes and take advantage of them

Now.

79-Thankful

For not? reaching my biggest goal

For my failures

Pains

Weaknesses

Misfortunes

Accomplishments

Suffering

Sickness

Health

Smiles

Children

Spouse

Family

Friends

Professors

And everything that God sends

My way

80-Something historical

Mark in your soul

Immortal in your feelings

Its importance is an admirable inspiration

Its blue prints

Are tattoos

In everything you are

81- Before is too late

Action of the now

Is the present moment

Make a combination

Of body, mind, spirit, soul, and heart

Your fears and your weaknesses

Will have to be

Your strengths

82- Clear or not

Communicate precisely

Detail for detail

Take everything in consideration

Like that your actions will be based

In judgments or designs

83- Confusion

Darkness mix with light

Undecided feelings

Is your ignorant wisdom

Is your frozen fire

Use your most effective technique

Then measure the result

If it coordinates with your purpose

You defeated confusion

84-Free will

Important in the result

That was or will be

Decision in our reach

Is a combination

Of motivation and inspiration

Let it live and revive

85- Honesty

Huge value and incomparable

It's worth more than fame, power, and money

To always perform it it's the purpose

This will take you close to the perfection

That only belongs

To God

86-I believe in your heart

With all our strengths

Let's believe is good

That its intentions are pure

We will not give up because of bad judgment

Which normally brings bad actions

honestly believe in that heart

We know and feel.

87- In lows with us

Never forget

What they done for us

Especially

When we were in the floors

For reasons of the destiny

Our times to recompense

Has to come

In the name

Of gratitude

88-Moment of love

Let's have faith and hope

That it will come

When it comes

Grab into it

With everything you are

Physically, mentally, and spiritually

You failed yesterday

When your moment of love comes

Do not fail

89-Observe my truth

With my pains

Weaknesses and adversities

Observe my truth

God already knows it

It signifies everything to me

That you

Know it

90-Special day

For one reason or other you worth much

The food is super delicious

The air is fresher

Enthusiasm is immense

Smiles are constant

The body, mind, heart

Have chemistry

Every second is appreciated

Tears are of pure joy

To wait for you

Is a tradition

91- Step of righteous faith

God

Guide us

Towards the just

In direction of good

For us and others

92-The childhood

Beautiful and unforgettable times

Sometimes they have dark moments

In general marvelous

With innocence given by the Creator

They are temporal moments

With objectives and supreme rights

To happy conditions

They pose divine energy

Demonstrated by their activities

Faith in children

93-The negotiator

Says

The good is expensive

Buys cheap and sells expensive

Do not let him/ her give you silver

Instead of white gold

The negotiator

Is not lying to you

Is part of the game,

And you are playing it

We have to respect him/her

They are working

94-The rich poverty

For having little and needing little

You have in abundance

You are ok without materialism

You are rich spiritually

Conformity is your costume

You value the little you have and the details of life

While the one that has a lot

Wants more and have imaginaries ambitions

For accepting your reality

You are a poor rich

95-To have power

Giant blessing

Which brings authority

To be able to help

The emergencies of others

In any type of conditions

To bring development is an obligation

Of ethics, justice, and humanism

96-Trap in love

Imagine that you are not if you want

But in reality

What you feel is the result

To be profoundly in love

Your heart was

A bait

Of love

97-Without understanding

Life is so much

Without compromise

Of intentions

Appearances

Actions and reality

We are in an abstract world

Harmful of our reality

98-You gave me strengths

The gratitude

Is internal, honest, and authentic

So real like our own existence

God gave you your strengths

You to me

Thank you

99- Silence

100- Anthem of the undocumented in the United States

God wanted for us to be today and let's have faith we will soon say, we were

Approximately twelve millions of undocumented in the United States

It shows us the concept of equality is very weak if we analyze the present

It is also clear that once twelve millions of voices unite

Haughty sound will humbly be

Powerful and historic like one day the Roman Empire

We pray to our God

To unite twelve millions of souls

Undocumented of the world race

Once the spirits are united we gave each other a hand brothers and sisters

Possibly with eternal faith

In God

Morsy's Vision of Hope Books
New York

Made in the USA
Middletown, DE
28 June 2015